How To Generate Leads
For Your Small Business

Proven strategies To Turn Strangers
Into High Paying Customers
Leveraging On Social Media

By

Sandra Jakes

TABLE OF CONTENT

Introduction

The success of small businesses in the vast digital environment of the 21st century depends on their ability to adapt, connect and thrive.

In this e-book, we travel to the heart of modern entrepreneurship and explore a fundamental but often difficult aspect of growing a business: lead generation.

How to Generate Leads for your Small Business is a comprehensive guide on how to navigate the ever-changing digital world.

The plan is to harness the incredible potential of social media, content marketing, and modern digital strategies to turn strangers into high-paying customers.

In this age of communication, your audience isn't just locals.It is global.

Your prospects are not right in front of you.

It only takes one click.If you understand the strategies and tactics required for effective lead generation, it is possible to reach these individuals, engage them and convert them into loyal customers.

This ebook will guide you through the difficult journey of understanding your target audience, building a strong online presence, creating compelling content, and mastering the art of social media advertising.

You'll learn how to connect with your audience, measure progress, and optimize your lead generation efforts for long-term success.

Whether you're a seasoned entrepreneur looking to improve your digital marketing strategy or a new business owner looking for guidance in the complex world of lead generation, this e-book is your trusted companion. We provide practical insights, and actionable steps to transform your small business into a manufacturing powerhouse.

Chapter 1

Overview Of Lead Generation

The digital age has changed the way companies communicate with their potential customers.

In today's environment, small business lead generation is no longer just an option.

It is essential for survival and growth.

This ebook is a comprehensive guide to understanding the strategies and tactics to use the power of social media to turn strangers into high-paying customers.

The importance of lead generation:
Lead generation is the process of identifying and attracting people or companies who are interested in your product or service. These people are not just random people.

These are potential customers who are genuinely interested in what you have to offer.

The importance of lead generation for small businesses is as follows:

Sustainability: Leaders are the lifeblood of any business. These are potential customers who will support and grow your business over time. Without a steady stream of leads, your business can stagnate or fail.

Cost-Effective: Lead generation is often more cost-effective than acquiring customers through traditional advertising or outbound marketing.

By focusing on people who are interested in your niche, you save valuable resources.

Targeted Marketing: Unlike mass marketing, which targets a broad audience, lead generation allows you to focus your efforts on specific market segments. This leads to higher conversion rates and ROI.

Build your brand: Successful lead generation increases brand awareness and trust.Providing valuable content and solutions to your audience will build your brand's reputation in the industry.

Increase Sales: Ultimately, the goal of lead generation is to increase sales. By nurturing leads and converting them into customers, you can grow your customer base and increase sales.

Why social media?

Social media has revolutionized the way we interact, communicate and do business.
This isn't just a place to share personal stories or cat videos.
It is a dynamic and growing market.

Here's why using social media to generate leads is a game changer.

Massive Audience: Social media platforms have billions of active users.

No other channel offers such a large and diverse pool of potential customers.

Targeting Options: Social media platforms offer very advanced targeting options.
You can use demographics, interests, behavior and more.Based on this, you can reach your ideal customers.

Participation and interaction: Social media is based on participation and conversation.
This helps you build meaningful relationships with your prospects and guide them through their buyer's journey.

Cost-effective advertising: Social media advertising can be budget-friendly, especially compared to traditional advertising methods.Even with a limited budget, you can reach a significant audience.

Analytics and Insights: Social media platforms offer powerful analytics tools to help you monitor the performance of your lead generation efforts.This data-driven approach enables continuous improvement.

What to expect:

This ebook guides you through the entire process of using social media to generate leads for your small business.

You'll learn how to identify your audience, build a strong online presence, create valuable content, choose the right social media platforms, use paid advertising effectively, connect with your audience, and measure and optimize your efforts.

By the end of this eBook, you'll have a comprehensive understanding of how to use the power of social media to convert strangers into high-paying customers.

Unleash the potential of your small business and prepare to enter a new era of growth and success.

Chapter 2
Understanding Your Target Audience

Understanding your target audience is the foundation of successful lead generation.

To effectively convert strangers into paying customers through social media, you first need to have a clear understanding of who your audience is.

Take a closer look at why this step is important and how you can fix it.

Why it's important to understand your target audience:

Relevance: Understanding your audience allows you to tailor your messages, content and offers to their specific needs, pain points and desires.This relevance increases the likelihood of communication and conversion.

Efficiency: Targeted marketing is more efficient.Instead of casting a wide net and hoping to collect a few leads, focus your resources and efforts on the people most likely to become paying customers.

Brand Trust: People trust companies that "get" them. When you demonstrate a deep understanding of your audience, you build trust, a key ingredient in converting leads.

Competitive Advantage: Understanding your target audience

can help you identify gaps in the market and create a unique selling proposition that sets you apart from your competitors.

How to understand your target audience:

Create a buyer persona: A buyer persona is a detailed representation of your ideal customer.This includes demographics, job roles, pain points, goals and even personal interests.To create these personas, start by analyzing your existing customer data and conducting market research.

Surveys and feedback: Contact existing customers and conduct surveys or interviews.Ask about their preferences, challenges and why they chose the company. This feedback can be invaluable in understanding your audience.

Social Listening: Use social media listening tools to monitor conversations about your industry, product or service. This allows you to understand what your target group is discussing and how they feel.

Competitive Analysis: Research your competitors.Who will they target and how?
What are the strengths and weaknesses of their approach?
This can give you clues about the common characteristics of your prospects.

Google Analytics and website data: to analyze the behavior of website visitors. What pages do you visit the most?What keywords are you using to find your site?
This data can reveal the interests and intentions of the public.

Join the conversation on social media. Participate in discussions on social media platforms relevant to your industry.Connect with potential leads and hear their opinions and questions.

Keyword research: Use tools like Google Keyword Planner to identify search terms and phrases used by your target audience. This helps with content creation and SEO.

A/B testing: Experiment with different marketing approaches and messages to see what works best for your audience. This data-driven approach can help you improve your understanding.

Understanding your target audience often requires segmentation.
This means dividing the audience into smaller groups based on common characteristics.
For example, different customer segments may have different buyer personas. Segmentation enables

personalized marketing efforts and better customer engagement.

Once you have a good understanding of your target audience, you are ready to move forward with the lead generation process.

Chapter 3
Building A Strong Online Presence

A strong online presence is essential to building a successful leader in the digital age.

Your small business's digital storefront is the first place potential customers encounter your brand.

In this chapter, we'll look at the importance of a strong online presence and how to build one effectively.

The importance of a strong network presence:

Credibility: An attractive and well-maintained online presence adds credibility to your business.Prospects will be more likely to trust your brand when they find a professional website and active social media profiles.

Feature: Your online presence is available 24/7 so potential customers can learn more about your company, product or service at their leisure. This accessibility is important in the lead generation process.

Visibility: A strong online presence increases visibility in the digital environment.You want people to be able to find you easily when they search for products or services related to your business.

Presence: Your online presence gives you a platform to interact with potential customers.You can build relationships with your audience through blog posts, social media updates, and interactions.

How to build a strong online presence:

Professional website:
Your website is your digital headquarters.
It should be visually appealing, easy to navigate and mobile friendly.
Optimize your website for search engines (SEO) to increase your visibility in search results.
Include informative content about your company, products, services, and contact information.

Sustainable branding:

Ensure consistent branding across all online platforms.

This includes your website, social media profiles and other digital touchpoints.

Use popular logos, color schemes and tone of voice.

Content creation:

Create high-quality, valuable content relevant to your target audience.

Publish blog posts, articles, videos, and other content that addresses your audience's needs and interests.

Presence in social networks:

Create and maintain active social media profiles on platforms relevant to your audience.

Post regularly, engage with your followers and share content that sparks discussion.

Online reviews and opinions:

Encourage satisfied customers to leave positive reviews on platforms like Google My Business or Yelp.

Display these reviews prominently on your website.

Email Advertising:

Build your email list by offering incentives such as e-books, newsletters or exclusive offers.

Send regular, relevant and engaging email content to your subscribers.

Online advertising:

To increase your online presence, consider using paid online advertising. Platforms like Google Ads and social media advertising can be effective for generating leads.

Watch and answer:

Use tools like Google Alerts or social media monitoring software to monitor mentions and discussions about your brand.

Respond quickly to comments, questions and feedback and demonstrate your commitment to customer engagement.

Local SEO:

If your small business relies on local customers, it's important to optimize your online presence for local searches.

Make sure your business information, including your name, address and phone number (NAP), is consistent across all online directories and platforms.

Claim and optimize your Google My Business listing to appear in local search results.

Mobile Optimization:

As the use of mobile devices increases, it is important that your online activities are mobile friendly.

Responsive website design, fast load times and easy navigation on mobile devices are important.

Remember that building a strong online presence is an ongoing effort. It requires constant updates, new content and constant communication with the audience.

Chapter 4
Content Marketing And Lead Magnet

Content marketing and lead magnets are powerful tools to attract and capture leads for your small business.
In this chapter, we'll take a closer look at these concepts and discuss how you can improve your lead generation efforts.

Content Marketing:
Content marketing is the strategic creation and distribution of valuable and relevant content to attract and engage a specific audience.
This plays an important role in generating leads for several reasons.

Educate and inform: Content marketing allows you to educate potential customers about your industry, products and services.
By providing valuable information, you position your brand as an authority in your niche.

Build Trust: Consistently producing high-quality content that addresses your audience's needs and pain points builds trust.
People engage more with brands they trust and ultimately buy from.

Increased Visibility: Content marketing improves your visibility online.
High-quality content that is optimized for search engines can rank higher in

search results, increasing the likelihood that potential customers will find your business.

Leads: Content marketing can move customers through the buyer's journey. Different types of content can be tailored to each stage, from initial awareness to consideration and decision making.

Key elements of effective content marketing include:

Blogging: Publish regular blog posts on topics relevant to your audience. These posts can answer frequently asked questions, offer solutions to problems, and showcase your expertise.

Video: Create video content such as tutorials, product demos and informational videos.
Video is a highly engaging format that helps you build strong relationships with your audience.

eBooks and White Papers: As a lead magnet, we offer in-depth guides, eBooks and white papers (more details coming soon). These resources may be helpful in lieu of contact information.

Infographics: Visual content like infographics simplify complex information and make it easy to share on social media.

Webinars and Podcasts: Host webinars and podcasts to connect with your audience in real time, share knowledge, and answer questions.

E-Newsletter: Send regular newsletters to your subscribers with updates, helpful tips and exclusive offers.

Lead Magnet:
A lead magnet is an incentive offered to a potential customer in exchange for contact information (usually an email

address). Lead magnets are an important part of the lead generation process because they help you get customers who are genuinely interested in your product or service.
Here are some examples of lead magnets:

eBooks and Textbooks: Comprehensive resources that provide valuable information on specific topics.
Example: "The Definitive Guide to Social Media Marketing for Small Businesses."

Checklists and Cheat Sheets: Provide checklists or cheat sheets to simplify the process or provide a quick reference guide.

Templates and Tools: Share templates, tools or calculators that make your audience's job easier.

An example would be a budget program for personal financial services.

Webinars and Workshops: Invite your prospects to a webinar or workshop that provides valuable information and solutions.

Case studies: Showcase real-life success stories or examples of how your products and services have helped customers.

Quizzes and Assessments: Provides interactive quizzes or assessments that provide personalized recommendations.

Discounts or exclusive offers: Offer discounts or exclusive offers to your subscribers or lead magnet downloaders.

Here's how the lead magnet process works:

Promotion: Promote your lead magnet on your website, social media and other marketing channels.
Explain the value your lead magnet provides.

Landing page: Create a custom landing page where potential customers can sign up instead of a lead magnet.

This page should be optimized for conversions.

Email Capture: Collect contact information (usually email addresses) from subscribers.

Delivery: Email your lead magnet to your subscribers or direct them to a download page.

Nurture and convert: Once you capture leads, you can increase conversion rates by nurturing them through email marketing and targeted content.

Adding content marketing and lead magnets to your lead generation strategy will greatly improve your small business's ability to attract and retain customers who are genuinely interested in what you have to offer.

Chapter 5
Social Media Platforms For Lead Generation

Choosing the right social media platform for lead generation is an important step in your small business's digital marketing strategy.

Each platform offers unique features and audiences, and choosing the platform that works best for you can have a huge impact on your lead generation efforts.

In this chapter, we'll look at the best social media platforms and their role in generating leads.

1.Facebook:

With more than 2.8 billion monthly active users, Facebook is the leading universal platform.
Our diverse user base allows us to target different demographics.

Lead Generation Tools: Facebook offers a lead generation form that allows users to submit contact information directly through the platform.
These forms can be used in advertising to effectively attract customers.

Content Strategy: Reach your target audience using engaging posts, videos and paid ads. Share valuable content, run contests and promote to attract leads.

*2. Instagram:

With over 1 billion monthly users, Instagram has a strong presence among young people.
Suitable for companies with a very visual and attractive image.

Lead generation tools: Instagram also offers a lead generation form in your ads to make it easy for users to indicate interest in your product or service.

Content strategy: Focus on visually appealing content, use storytelling through Instagram Stories, and collaborate with influencers to expand your reach.

3. LinkedIn:

LinkedIn is the best platform for B2B lead generation.

It has over 800 million users, mostly professionals and businesses.

Lead Generation Tools: LinkedIn offers Sponsored Content and Sponsored InMail for lead generation.

You can target specific positions, industries or companies.

Content Strategy: Share thought-leader content, industry insights and case studies.

Join relevant LinkedIn groups and connect with prospects via messaging.

4. Twitter:

Audience: Twitter has approximately 400 million users.
It is a live chat platform and can be useful for businesses targeting a broad or tech-savvy audience.

Lead Generation Tools: Twitter lead generation cards allow you to collect leads directly from your promoted tweets.

Content Strategy: Use hashtags to increase visibility, participate in industry conversations, and post links to valuable content.

*5. Pinterest:
Pinterest is a visual platform with over 400 million monthly users, the majority of whom are women.

It is suitable for companies that provide visual products or services.

Lead Generation Tool: Pinterest allows you to create pins with a call-to-action (CTA) that links to a landing page where users can submit information.

Content Strategy: Create visual pins that showcase your product or service. Use rich pins and links to helpful blog posts or landing pages.

6. youtube:
With over 2 billion monthly users, YouTube is the second largest search engine in the world.
This is ideal for businesses that can produce video content.

Lead generation tools: Use video descriptions to add links to landing pages, lead capture forms or downloadable resources.

Content Strategy: Create informative and engaging videos tailored to the needs and interests of your target audience.
Add a powerful CTA to your video content.

*7. Snapchat
Snapchat primarily appeals to younger users, with approximately 500 million monthly active users.

Lead Generation Tools: Snapchat offers lead generation ads that help you capture leads through the platform.

Content Strategy: Connect with younger audiences using Snapchat's engaging features like Stories and Lenses.

Consider the following factors when choosing a social media platform for lead generation:

Audience demographics: Choose the platforms where your audience is most active.

Content Type: Focus on platforms that match the type of content you can create and share effectively.

Advertising options: Evaluate the availability of lead generation tools and paid advertising options on each platform.

Competitor Presence: Study where your competitors are operating and measure their success.

Resources: Think about the time and resources you can allocate to each platform.

Remember that your promotion on a few platforms is often more effective than your promotion on many platforms. Quality and consistency of approach are the keys to generating success in social media.

Chapter 6
Paid Social Media Advertising For Lead Generation

Paid social media advertising is a powerful lead generation tool for small businesses.

This allows you to reach your target group and get results quickly.

In this chapter, we explore the world of social media advertising and discuss the importance, strategies, and best practices for lead generation.

The Importance of Paid Social Media Advertising:

Precise targeting: Social media platforms offer advanced targeting options.
You can define your audience based on demographics, interests, behavior and even actual interactions with your brand.

Instant Visibility: Unlike organic efforts that take time to gain traction, paid advertising provides immediate visibility.Once you launch a campaign, your ads can be shown to your target audience.

Scalability: Paid advertising allows you to control your budget and scale your efforts as needed.

Whether your budget is small or large, strategic targeting can help you make the most of it.

Measurable Results: Social media advertising provides detailed analytics so you can track the performance of your campaigns.You can measure clicks, conversions and ROI from your lead generation efforts.

Paid Social Media Advertising Strategy:

Choose the right platform: Based on your audience research, choose the social media platforms your target audience is most active on. For example, a B2B company may find LinkedIn ads effective, and a visually appealing product may rank well on Instagram and Pinterest.

Set Clear Goals: Define your lead generation goals.
Want to capture email addresses, increase website traffic and encourage downloads from your lead magnet?
Setting clear goals will give you direction when creating your ad.

Creative and attractive design: Creativity is important. Use impressive images and compelling ad text that clearly communicates the value of your offer.
A strong call to action (CTA) is essential.

A/B testing: Experiment with different ad elements, including headlines, images, and ad content. A/B testing can help you decide what works best for your audience.

Landing page: Make sure the landing page that takes users to your ad is optimized for conversion.
Your ad should be relevant and provide a seamless experience.

Lead forms: If you're capturing leads through direct advertising, make sure your forms are clear and require minimal input.
Long forms can prevent users from taking action.

Remarketing: Implement a remarketing campaign to retarget users who previously engaged with your brand but did not convert.These users are more likely to become leads.

Budget allocation: Set a realistic budget for your advertising campaign. Allocate your budget based on the platforms and campaigns that perform best.

Ad scheduling: Schedule your ads to show when your audience is most active.
Social media platforms often offer scheduling options to optimize ad serving.

Conversion Tracking: Implement conversion tracking to track the performance of your lead generation campaigns.This helps you estimate the return on investment of your advertising efforts.

Best practices:

Use lead generation forms: Many social media platforms offer lead generation forms that users can fill out without leaving the platform.This reduces friction during the conversion process.

Quality Score: Platforms like Facebook and Google Ads use Quality Score to evaluate the relevance and quality of your ads and landing pages.A higher Quality Score means lower advertising costs and higher visibility.

Ad Coherence and Visual Consistency: Ensure consistency between your ad copy and images on your landing page. This reinforces your message and ensures that users are not confused or disappointed.

Mobile optimization: As mobile usage becomes more common, make sure your ads and landing pages are mobile-friendly.

Follow policies: Know the advertising policies of the social media platforms you use.Advertising campaigns that violate our policies may be fined or banned.

Paid social media advertising is a dynamic industry, so it's important to stay on top of platform updates and industry trends. Be prepared to adjust and improve your strategy based on performance data and feedback from your lead generation campaigns.

Chapter 7
Engaging Your Audience

Engaging your audience on social media is a critical step in the lead generation process.

This is where you can build relationships, build trust and convert leads into paying customers.

This chapter explores the importance of engaging and providing strategies to communicate effectively with audiences.

The importance of community involvement:

Building Rapport: Connecting with your audience is more than just delivering a message.

It's about building real connections and relationships.People are more likely to become customers when they feel a personal connection to your brand.

Trust and credibility: Regular and meaningful interaction with your audience helps build trust and credibility.
You can demonstrate your commitment to customer satisfaction by answering questions, providing valuable information, and resolving concerns.

Lead generation: Collaboration is the bridge between lead capture and conversion.We can help you connect with suppliers to guide them through their buyer's journey and give them the information and support they need.

Strategies for effective audience engagement:

 Reply to comments and messages: Respond instantly to comments on social media posts and messages from your audience.

Active:

Don't expect any interaction. I like content, sharing and selecting and actively contracting the public.

When they receive their message, they show that they are grateful for their contribution.

Host Q&A sessions and live chats.

Host a live Q&A or live chat where you can answer questions, share insights, and connect with your audience in real time.

share user-generated content:

Encourage your audience to create and share content related to your product or service.

Show your customers that you appreciate and value them by displaying user-generated content.

create surveys and polls:

Use surveys and polls to collect feedback and information from your audience.
This will not only keep your customers interested, but also give you valuable data to improve your offers.

Personalize your contacts:

If possible, name the target group. Personalized responses and interactions will make your audience feel valued and appreciated.

Tell the story behind the scenes and share your content.

Stories and behind-the-scenes content can humanize your brand and connect your audience with the people behind your company.

Join relevant groups and communities:

Join industry specific online groups and communities.
Participate in discussions, provide value and establish yourself as an expert in your field.

Share your valuable content:

Consistently deliver content that educates, informs, and entertains your audience.
This includes blog posts, videos, infographics, and more.
maybe.

Use social listening:
Use social listening tools to monitor conversations about your industry, brand and products.
This will help you understand what's being said and respond accordingly.

Consistency and Authenticity:
Consistency is the key to capturing your audience's attention.
Always communicate with your audience and maintain an honest and genuine tone in your interactions.

Authenticity builds trust, and consistency ensures that audiences know what to expect from your brand.

Measurement of activity indicators:
Track key metrics including likes, comments, shares and direct messages to measure the effectiveness of your engagement efforts. Track the growth of your social media followers, the reach of your posts, and the comments and sentiments of your posts.

Listen to feedback:
Feedback is a valuable source of insight.

Pay attention to positive or negative feedback from your audience. Use feedback to demonstrate your commitment to improving, solving problems, and meeting customer needs.

Public engagement is an ongoing process, not a one-time task.
It's about maintaining relationships and guiding leads through the conversion process.

Chapter 8
Measuring And Optimizing Your Lead Generation Efforts

Measuring and optimizing your lead generation efforts is critical to ensuring the growth and success of your small business. This chapter explores the importance of tracking progress, key metrics to monitor, and strategies for optimizing your lead generation process.

Importance of measurement:

Accountability: Measurement holds you accountable for your lead generation efforts.This will help you see what works and what doesn't so you can make informed decisions.

Continuous improvement: Tracking results helps you identify areas that need improvement.
This iterative process helps you refine your strategy and maximize your ROI.

Measure your ROI: Measuring your lead generation efforts can give you an idea of your ROI.This will help you allocate resources efficiently and justify your marketing budget.

Key indicators to measure:

Conversion Rate: The percentage of leads that become customers.

Calculate this by dividing the number of conversions by the total number of leads generated.

Cost Per Lead (CPL): The cost associated with acquiring each lead. Divide your total marketing costs by the number of leads generated.

Click-Through Rate (CTR): The percentage of people who click on your ad or content.
This is a measure of how engaging your content is with your audience.

Return on Investment (ROI): The return on your lead generation efforts compared to the total cost of those efforts.

Calculate this by subtracting expenses from income and dividing by expenses.

Lead quality: Assess lead quality based on criteria relevant to your business, including lead source, demographics, and behavior.

Conversion Funnel Metrics: Track key conversion funnel stages, including awareness, consideration, and decision stages.See where your leads land or convert.

Email metrics: If email marketing is part of your lead generation, track metrics like open rates, click-through rates, and conversion rates for your email campaigns.

Optimization strategy:

A/B Testing: Run continuous A/B tests to compare different elements of your lead generation efforts, including ad copy, visuals, landing page design, and CTAs. Make changes based on what works best for you.

Lead Nurturing: Improve your lead nurturing process by creating personalized content and email sequences that guide your prospects through the buyer's journey.

Remarketing: If users don't convert on the first interaction, run a remarketing campaign to get them to re-engage with relevant content or offers.

Segmentation: Segment customers based on demographics, behavior and other criteria.This allows for personalized and targeted lead nurturing.

Content Optimization: We regularly update and optimize our content to ensure relevance and effectiveness in attracting and growing leads.

Budget allocation: Allocate your budget to the best performing campaigns and channels. Continually evaluate which campaigns produce the highest ROI.

Integrate feedback: Gather feedback from your sales team and customers and make data-driven improvements to your lead generation efforts.

Competitive Analysis: Analyze your competitors' lead generation strategies to identify opportunities and gaps in your own efforts.

Data-driven decision making:
Your lead generation process needs to be data-driven. Regularly review analytics and performance data to

guide informed decisions and
optimization efforts.

Reference system settings:
Establish benchmarks based on your
industry and business goals.
These benchmarks provide a baseline
for evaluating the success of your lead
generation efforts.

Documentation and reporting:
Document your strategy, results, and
optimization efforts.
Regular reporting ensures
accountability and transparency within
the organization.

Repeat and improve:

Remember that optimization is an ongoing process.What works today may not work tomorrow.Continually evaluate your lead generation efforts and adapt to audience, industry and technology changes.

By measuring, optimizing and improving your lead generation strategy, you can achieve better results over time and continuously adapt to the changing digital marketing landscape.

Remember, measuring and optimizing takes effort, but can reap significant rewards in terms of lead generation and increased revenue.

Conclusion

When you finish this How to Lead Generation for your Small Business eBook, you will be embarked on a transformative journey into the dynamic world of digital marketing and lead generation.

You learned the ins and outs of understanding your audience, building a strong online presence, creating compelling content, mastering social media advertising techniques, connecting with your audience, and measuring and optimizing your lead generation efforts.

Now, as you reflect on your learnings and strategies, it's important to recognize that lead generation isn't just a set task.

It is an ongoing process, dynamic mindset and plan. Your journey doesn't end here.

This is an ongoing adventure that evolves with your business, industry trends and technological advances.

Your small business can achieve incredible growth through effective lead generation.
It is a journey full of opportunities, challenges and moments of triumph.

As you apply the insights and strategies in this e-book, remember that lead generation success depends not only on the quantity of leads, but also on their quality.

With dedication, persistence, and the knowledge you gain, you'll be equipped to navigate the ever-evolving digital landscape and turn strangers into high-paying clients. This e-book is your guide, resource and companion on this exciting journey.

So, take the reins of your small business and enter the world of lead generation with confidence and purpose.

We hope you apply what you learn to help your business thrive, your clients grow, and your entrepreneurial dreams come true.The success of your small business and the bright future you create are here to stay.

www.ingramcontent.com/pod-product-compliance
Lightning Source LLC
Chambersburg PA
CBHW061004260726
48661CB00005B/2052